KT-460-259

ASK ISAAC ASIMOV ?

# How do aeroplanes fly?

Heinemann

First published in Great Britain by Heinemann Library
an imprint of Heinemann Publishers (Oxford) Ltd
Halley Court, Jordan Hill, Oxford OX2 8EJ

OXFORD LONDON EDINBURGH MADRID
ATHENS BOLOGNA PARIS MELBOURNE
SYDNEY AUCKLAND SINGAPORE TOKYO
IBADAN NAIROBI HARARE GABORONE
PORTSMOUTH NH (USA)



98 97 96 95 94

10 9 8 7 6 5 4 3 2 1

**British Library Cataloguing in Publication Data is available from the British Library on request.**

ISBN 0 431 07648 0

Cover designed and pages typeset by Philip Parkhouse
Printed in China

**Picture Credits**

pp. 2-3, Courtesy of AMETEK, Inc.; pp. 4-5, © Picture Perfect USA; pp. 6-7, © Dick Poe/Visuals Unlimited; p. 6 (inset), © Mary Evans Picture Library; pp. 8-9, Courtesy of Special Collections and Archives, Wright State University; pp. 10-11, © Jon Allyn, Cr. Photogr., 1992; pp. 12-13, Kurt Carloni/Artisan, 1992; pp. 14-15 © Adams Picture Library; pp. 16-17, Kurt Carloni/Artisan, 1992; pp. 18-19, © Joseph Giannetti/Third Coast Stock Source; pp. 20-21, Courtesy of NASA; pp. 22-23, Kurt Carloni/Artisan, 1992; p. 24, Kurt Carloni/Artisan, 1992

Cover photograph © Hutchison Library
Back cover photograph © Sygma/D. Kirkland

The book designer wishes to thank Gift of Wings and the model for their cooperation.

Series editor: Valerie Weber
Editors: Barbara J. Behm and Patricia Lantier-Sampon
Series designer: Sabine Beaupré
Book designer: Kristi Ludwig
Picture researcher: Diane Laska

# Contents



Words that appear in the glossary are printed in **bold** the first time they occur in the text.

## Modern-day wonders

Pick up your telephone and talk to someone halfway round the world. Turn on your video-recorder and watch a television programme that was shown last night after you had gone to bed. These are only some of the many wonders of **technology**.

Air travel is another amazing achievement of our modern world. How do aeroplanes fly? Let's find out.

BRITISH AIRWAYS
G-BGDU
AIR FRANCE
Airbus

## Is flying easy?

Flying seems easy when we watch a seagull gliding overhead. But a bird must overcome two forces in order to soar through the air.

**Gravity** pulls everything towards the ground. **Air resistance** slows anything moving through the air. For hundreds of years people tried to overcome these natural forces. In the early 1900s, two brothers finally succeeded.

## When was the first aeroplane flight?

It was on 17 December 1903, in the USA at Kitty Hawk, North Carolina. Orville Wright stepped into a frail-looking machine, turned on the engine, and climbed aloft into full flight. With this first twelve-second ride, Orville and Wilbur Wright made history.

The Wright brothers used two types of power to get their plane into the air. **Thrust** propelled the plane forwards. **Lift** pulled it up into the air. Without these forces, no plane can fly. Orville and Wilbur Wright influenced world aviation for many years after Kitty Hawk. They built flying machines in the USA and Europe.

## What is the Bernoulli effect?

The thrust of a plane's engine helps the plane to achieve lift, which carries the plane into the air. These two forces make flight possible because of the **Bernoulli effect**.

Air flowing over a surface changes the **air pressure** on that surface. The faster the air flows, the lower the pressure. This is called the Bernoulli effect. You can see how this works if you blow over a strip of paper. The strip rises because pressure decreases over the paper as you blow.

## Why are aeroplane wings curved?

As a plane takes off, the Bernoulli effect becomes important. The diagrams show how the wings split the air into two streams. The curved shape of the wings forces the air to flow more quickly over the upper surface than under the lower surface. This decreases the air pressure on the upper surface because of the Bernoulli effect. So the wings are lifted up by the greater pressure beneath the wings, carrying the plane into the air.

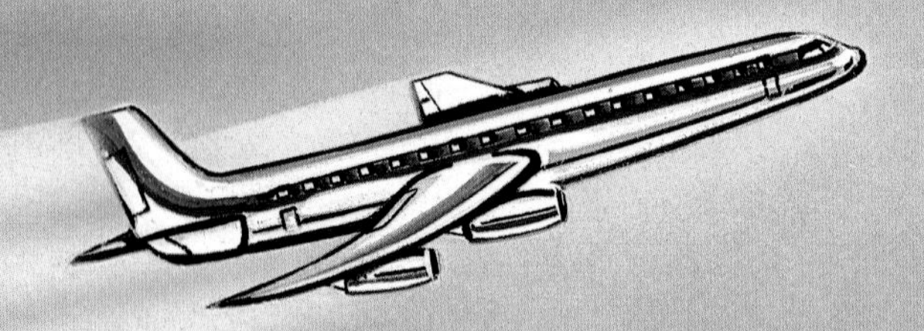

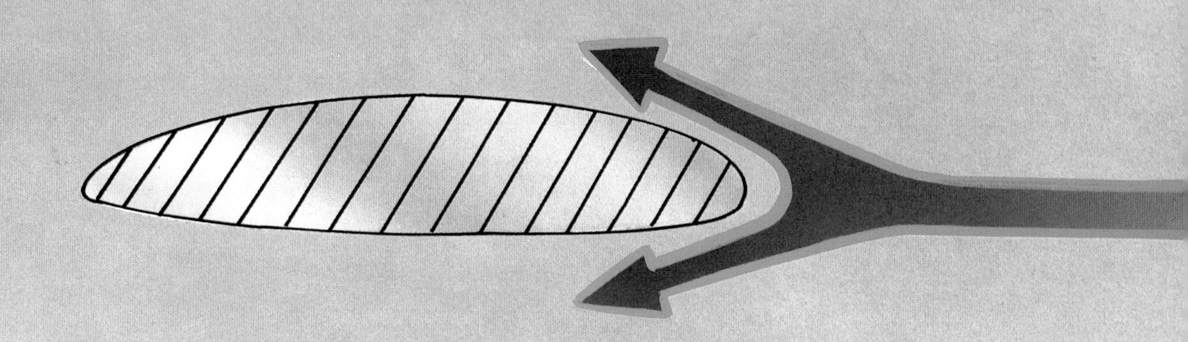

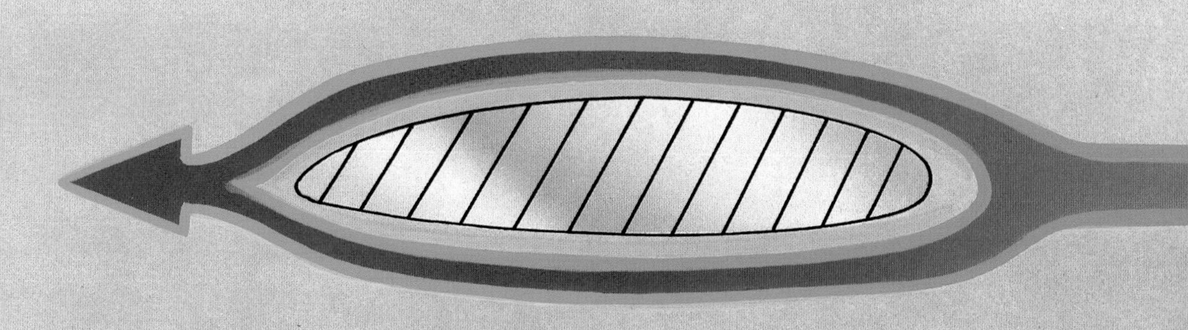

## What are the engines for?

A strong air current can lift a plane, but we cannot always rely on wind power. A more reliable way to make air flow across the wings is to move the wings forward through the air. This is the job of the plane's

engines. A plane's engines drive the plane down the runway. Once in flight, the engines keep the plane moving through the air. Without this forward thrust, the plane would not be able to stay in the air.

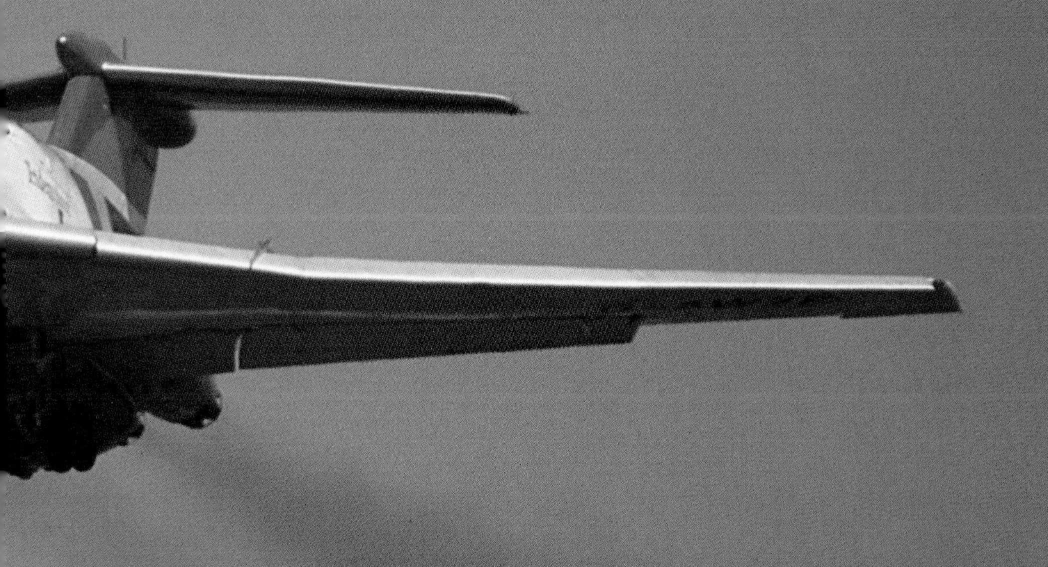

## What is the difference between propellers and jet engines?

Planes obtain thrust from either propellers or jet engines. The spinning propeller makes air move faster in front of the propeller than behind it. This lowers the air pressure in front

of the plane. The plane moves forwards. With a jet, air flows into the engine. The air is **compressed** and combined with fuel. A spark ignites the fuel and air mixture. The exploding gases escape from the back of the engine, thrusting the plane forwards.

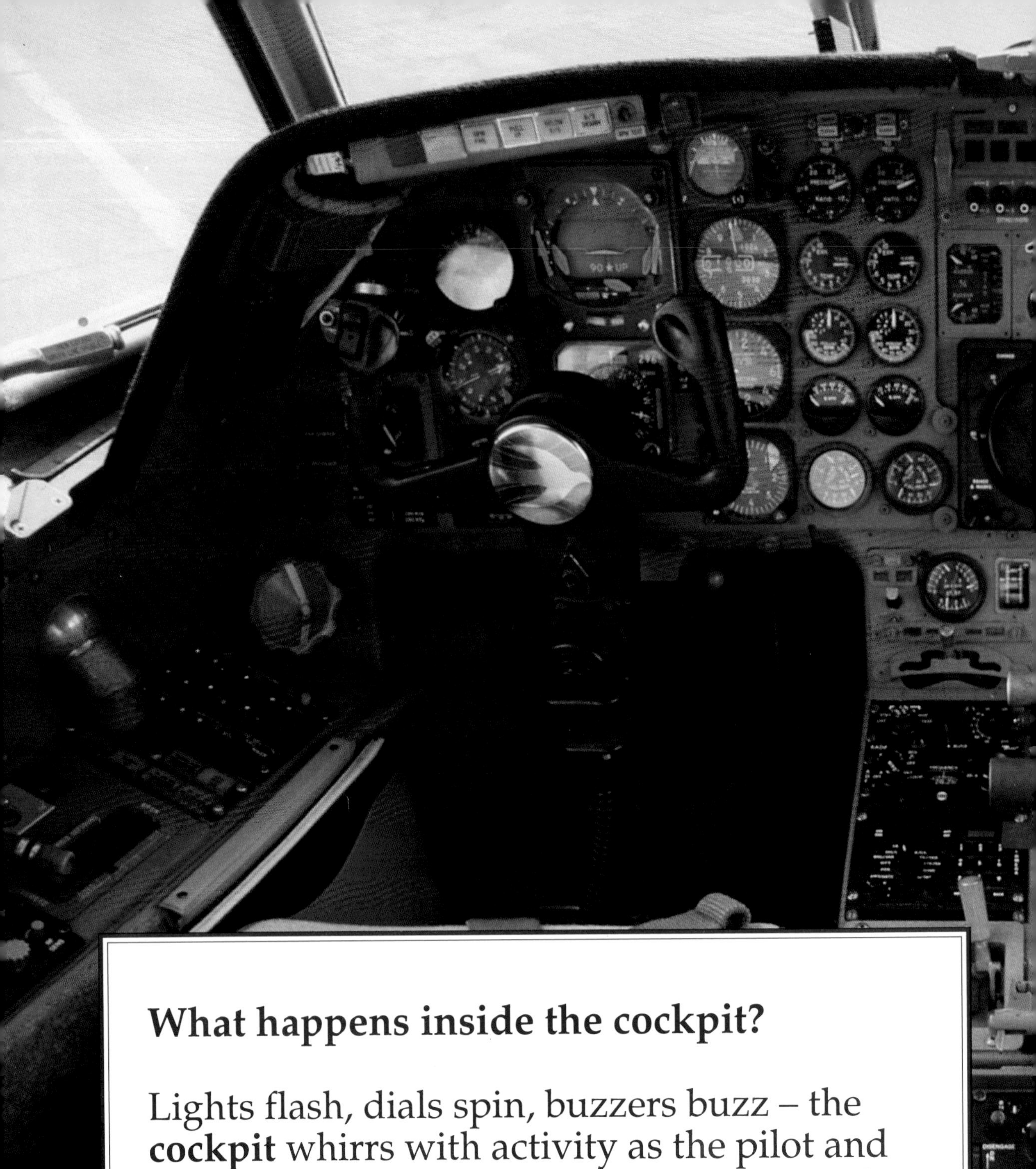

## What happens inside the cockpit?

Lights flash, dials spin, buzzers buzz – the **cockpit** whirrs with activity as the pilot and copilot prepare for take-off. They set switches and watch the instruments all around them. These instruments keep track of the plane's

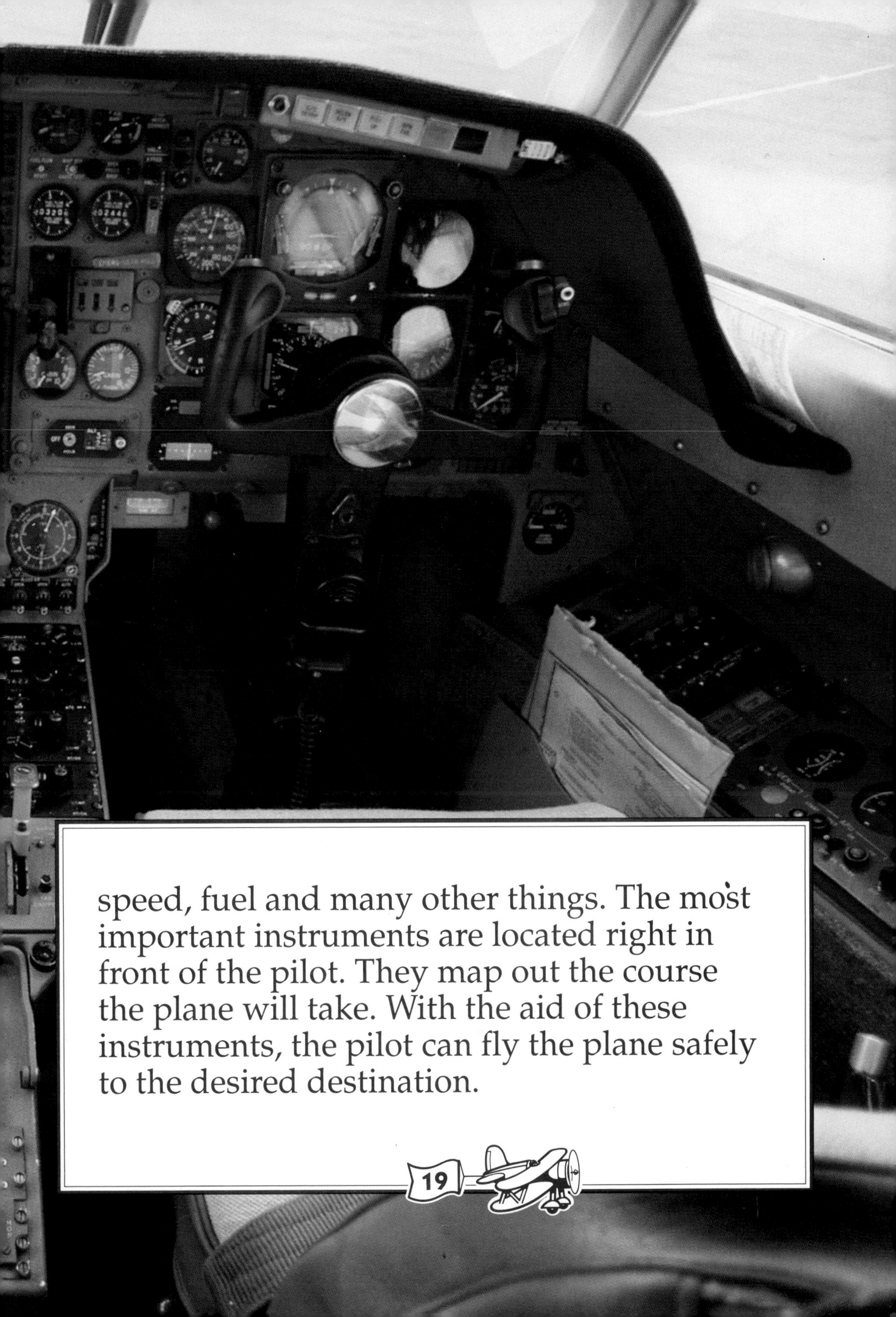

speed, fuel and many other things. The most important instruments are located right in front of the pilot. They map out the course the plane will take. With the aid of these instruments, the pilot can fly the plane safely to the desired destination.

## Is the space shuttle an aeroplane?

Some planes go up into space and **orbit** the Earth. The **space shuttle** is a combined spacecraft and aeroplane which is launched from a rocket. Astronauts use the shuttle to repair **satellites** and perform experiments. Then they fly the shuttle back to Earth. The shuttle glides down through the clouds at high speeds. It needs an extra long runway to land safely. Afterwards, the shuttle can be launched into space again.

NASA
United States

## What lies in the future?

Aeroplanes are so common that it is hard to believe they were once an impossible dream. But one day our jets may seem as old-fashioned as a horse and cart. In the future we may fly in sun-powered planes or jump into a mini-plane to go to work. The future of flight is as limitless as the sky.

# Glossary

**air pressure:** the force that air exerts on anything it touches

**air resistance:** the friction caused by air rubbing against anything that moves through it

**Bernoulli effect:** the decrease in air pressure that results when air movement increases

**cockpit:** the cabin in an aeroplane where the pilot and copilot sit

**compressed:** forced to occupy a smaller space

**gravity:** the force that pulls everything towards the Earth

**lift:** the force that causes an aeroplane's wings to move upwards

**orbit:** to circle a planet or star

**satellite:** an object or vehicle that circles any celestial body such as the Earth or the Moon. Satellites can receive and transmit television, radio and other signals.

**space shuttle:** the reusable spacecraft that lands on a runway in the same way that an aeroplane does

**technology:** the use of scientific principles to produce things which are useful to people

**thrust:** the force that causes a plane to move forwards through the air

# Index